SUMMARY OF
THE ENERGY BUS

10 Rules to Fuel Your Life, Work, and
Team with Positive Energy

A Guide To Jon Gordon's Book

Flawless Summaries

<u>DISCLAIMER</u>

Table of Contents

Introduction

How would you grade your overall life right now, on a scale of 1 to 10? Some people may find it to be quite high, while others will find it to be quite low. Nevertheless, regardless of the score you gave yourself, at some moment or another, all of us are going to experience an energy dip.

Jon Gordon is a well-known motivational speaker, author, and expert in the fields of teamwork, leadership, and sales in the United States. The Wall Street Journal bestseller, The Energy Bus, examines the difficulties that people face daily and provides advice on how to overcome those difficulties.

In this article, we will go over the ten basic guidelines that, if followed, will lead you on the adventure of a lifetime. Put on your safety belt and climb aboard the energy shuttle.

Meet George

In this straightforward metaphor, George takes on the role of the everyman figure.

At the lightbulb factory where George works, he is in middle management. Because of his reliable income, he has a wonderful life in the suburbs. He has a wonderful home, the financial means to purchase brand-new automobiles, and the ability to provide for his family. On the other hand, George isn't exactly content.

George has been experiencing a rising period in which he finds himself increasingly dissatisfied, to the point that both his employer and his wife give him ultimatums to choose from. If he doesn't adjust the way he thinks, he'll end up getting fired from his job and divorced from his wife.

When this occurs, things start to get incredibly chaotic at work, and the situation gets even worse when his car breaks down and he has to take the bus to work because he has no other option. As soon as George managed to squeeze himself onto the #11 bus, the ecstatic driver, Joy, greeted him. Joy is unfazed by George's tumultuous disposition, and she explains to him that it is her responsibility to "invigorate passengers." Joy is an "energy ambassador" who encourages others to think positively and gives ten principles for having "the ride of your life."

Having a constructive and goal-oriented way of life is the driving force behind The Energy Bus. It is not about having surface motivations or seeming to be enthusiastic while being dishonest. The goal is to develop a life that is full of energy and optimism for the future while simultaneously embracing the positive, avoiding those that drain your energy, sometimes known as "energy vampires," and weeding out such people.

Day One

George acquires an essential piece of knowledge on the very first day, which is that he is the one who drives. Because we are all in command of our destinies, none of us can point the finger of blame at another person for the way our lives turn out. When it comes to accepting responsibility for our lives and the choices we make, a lot of us fall short. We need to celebrate not just our victories but also our setbacks.

How much of your life is shaped by the decisions and actions of other people?

You can make changes in your life if you are living by what other people are asking you to do or if you are acting in a way that does not seem authentic to you. We each can make our own decisions, and we must settle on whether or not we will be the captains of our buses. By the conclusion of the first day, George has realized that the greatest gift we are given is the freedom and power to make choices and that once we begin to take responsibility for our own lives, everything shifts, and changes.

As the driver of our bus, not only do we get to pick whether we spend our time with individuals who have low or high energy, but we also get to select whether we consume meals that give us energy or those that don't. Every choice we make has an effect not just on ourselves but also on the others in our immediate environment. Because of this, even as simple as smiling at or acknowledging another person can have a big effect.

Day Two

On the second day of the trip, Joy reminds George to keep his attention on the voyage. It is one thing to become aware that you are in the driver's seat, but it is another entirely to be aware of your destination.

Where do you plan on going, and what exactly do you want to see while you're there? What kind of world do you want to make for yourself and the others in your immediate environment?

Getting to grips with our goals for the future could appear to be an overwhelming task. You should make an effort to start by concentrating on your goals for yourself, then broaden these goals to include what you want from your professional life and the people you work with, and last, how you want your relationships to be.

When we are startled by something or someone, we frequently spring into action and begin working toward the realization of our vision. It could be that we look in the mirror and don't like what we see, it could be that someone tells us a harsh reality about ourselves, or it could be that we find ourselves in a situation where we need to make a difficult decision. In any case, we should all direct our attention toward our objectives to be aware of the course that we are following.

People who have read The Secret are likely familiar with the concept of the law of attraction. According to the principle known as the law of attraction, if we apply sufficient concentration and effort, we can bring something into our life. This article contends that we can bring more happiness into our lives by employing various strategies for envisioning it. In addition, the assumption is that if we concentrate our efforts on material goods, our welfare, and our possibilities, we will be able to benefit from them in the future.

The Third Day

How can one have a happy attitude when everything in their immediate environment appears to be falling apart?

On day three, Joy argues that to alter your existing circumstances, you need to change how you think about those circumstances. E plus P equals O is the change formula that she offers, which is quite helpful.

Let's take this and dissect it. The letter E is for "events," and the letter P is for "perception." The letter O represents the final result. The central thesis of this book is that although we cannot control external events, we can alter the way we see them. Therefore, when you are confronted with an incident, have a positive attitude about it, and you will affect the outcome.

For instance, if you are asked to the party of one of your previous partners, you would consider this to be a nightmarish scenario. If, on the other hand, you reinterpret this circumstance as an opportunity to socialize with new people while also having a wonderful time, you will have a better chance of changing the outcome while also having more fun. In a similar vein, if you see that

15

there is a work meeting set for the wee hours of the morning on Monday, you might think of it as an opportunity to present a fresh concept that could affect the entire working week. As a result, rather than dreading the meeting, you might even find yourself looking forward to it.

The Fourth, Fifth, And Sixth Days

The significance of persuading other individuals to board the bus was brought home to us on day four as the day's takeaway lesson.

Because it is necessary for a team to be in step with one another, it is necessary to encourage "buy-in" from each member of the team. The first thing you need to do is communicate openly and honestly with the other members of your team, sharing both your vision and your objectives. After you have completed this step, it is up to them to determine whether or not they choose to ride the bus. It is vitally necessary for us to be aware of what we are agreeing to, as this plays a role in the formation of trust.

Day five might be challenging because on this day you find out who is getting on the bus with you, who is not coming on the bus, and who you need to push off the bus to make room for new passengers.

Did you know that according to a survey conducted by Gallup in 2013, seventy percent of American workers either despise their employment or are disengaged while on the job? Imagine that you are one of the thirty percent of workers who enjoy their jobs. Do you have any thoughts about the effect that being exposed to that much negativity would have on your performance? And while this isn't to imply that every company has a ratio of 70 percent of employees that exhibit negative behavior, given these figures, it's safe to assume that the consequences of the "energy vampire" are felt in the majority of companies.

The office is an expensive environment for negativity, and people who are consistently pessimistic deplete the vitality of those around them. On the sixth day of the challenge, George saw how important it is to get rid of members of a team who are working against the success of the group. Additionally, it is crucial to show appreciation for the customers who ride on your bus. Because of your previous actions or because you haven't acknowledged them, there is a possibility that some people will be reluctant to join you. As a result, you should make certain that you open up clear channels of communication so that everyone has the opportunity to communicate how they feel and any difficulties that they might have.

Seventh And Eighth Days Of The Week

George had a breakthrough in his understanding of leadership on days seven and eight.

First, it is made clear to him that to be an effective leader, one must lead from the heart. Joy gives him the piece of advice that it is not enough to simply hold the position of CEO; instead, he needs to hold the position of "chief energy officer."

The level of energy present in a workplace is critical to the success of a firm. In addition, having an energizing work environment means that employees aren't afraid to learn new things or make mistakes. Opportunities are created when there is positive energy to drive them, and opportunities are the first step on the growth path.

Would you be willing to put in the extra effort to join a ground-breaking team if you were offered the chance to do so? The vast majority of us aspire to be a part of exceptional teams, and many of us are willing to take on even the most menial of responsibilities simply to be able to say that we were a member of such a team. The fact of the matter is that people want to be a part of teams that are both interesting and energized.

We need to lead by example and show excitement to build an energized team. A growing number of motivated individuals tends to generate excitement throughout a group because enthusiasm is infectious. However, one should not be excited in a dishonest or fake manner; rather, their excitement should originate from a place of dedication and vision.

However, George discovers on day eight that it is not sufficient to simply have a cheerful attitude and an eager outlook. Good leaders inspire their followers with affection and always have the team's success in mind while making decisions. When you lead with love, it communicates to your team that they are valued, and it creates an environment in which everyone feels liked and respected. Everyone ought to have the experience of being seen and heard.

People that work together in environments that have high levels of morale have a sense that they are cared for, and they also have a sense that their future is safe. In addition, they put forth their best effort since they have the perception that their superior qualities are appreciated. Importantly, it's not only about recognizing the qualities that individuals possess; it's also about putting those strengths to use and trusting people to excel in the areas in which they have experience.

Last but not least, set aside some time to familiarize yourself with the people around you and pay attention to what they have to say. Listening is one of the most important things a leader can do to demonstrate empathy, which is one of the most important talents displayed by a leader. In addition to this, leaders should acknowledge and celebrate significant milestones and successes, as well as give opportunities for people to showcase their best selves. A good leader is someone who not only serves the employees but also leads by example by going first.

Day Nine

What is your overarching goal?

We need to give much more consideration to the kind of legacy we wish to leave behind, and as a result, we should think about the people who are close to us. We need to investigate various views concerning our abilities and inquire into what others can learn from us.

Our overarching goal also serves as the objective of the team. Leaders are responsible for cultivating a culture of teamwork and value, one in which even the most menial tasks are acknowledged as essential.

According to Simon Sinek, a strong leader always begins with answering the question "why," because doing so motivates other people to invest in the initiative or enterprise. According to Gordon, having a purpose infuses your day-to-day life with a sense of passion.

Day Ten

On the tenth day of his travel, other passengers greet George by singing, "Too privileged to be stressed!"

Even though there is a lot of strife and difficulty in life, there is also an abundance of exceptional beauty, joy, and hope. This is a major but. Because this will be our only trip on the bus, we should make the most of it and not take anything for granted.

To begin, get rid of all of those insignificant worries and fears that have arisen as a result of being inconvenienced. When you look back on your life, the insignificant things won't matter to you at all. According to the author of this work, "After you die, your mailbox will continue receiving emails."

In a research study, participants who were 95 years old were asked what activities they wished they had engaged in more frequently throughout their long lives. Unsurprisingly, none of them desired any further rice cakes to consume. But, in all seriousness, the top responses were on living in the present now, being more conscious, reflecting more, taking greater risks, and leaving a legacy.

Remember that we leave our histories and the good energy that we've generated behind us.

A Brand-New George

George was able to completely transform his life when he paid attention to and followed the ten guidelines.

No matter who we are, there are things that we can all take away from George's life. The phrase "feed the positive dog" is often cited as one of the most meaningful messages. Two dogs are living inside of each one of us: the one that is hostile and aggressive, and the other that is kind and optimistic. We give food to the dog who has the most command over the pack. Therefore, if we continue to foster positive, it will eventually come to predominate and triumph.

We may provide nourishment for our positive pets by adopting an optimistic outlook and demonstrating gratitude. One of the most beneficial ways to express thankfulness is to keep a gratitude journal in which one records one thing each night before going to bed. Keeping these upbeat thoughts in mind helps us to maintain our concentration on what matters.

Developing meaningful relationships with other people, whether they be family members, coworkers, teammates, or classmates, is yet another constructive thing you can do. Invite folks on board the bus, and then tell them what you anticipate from them once they get there. Encourage these individuals to talk to one another, but keep in mind that not everyone will be interested in hopping on the energy bus. This is OK, but you need to determine who these people are so that you can avoid letting them drain your energy. The so-called "energy vampires" have to be found and exposed before we can get away from them. If there are people on your team who are sucking your team's energy dry, those people either need to change their attitude or quit the team.

Conclusion

The energy bus is not simply about us; rather, it is also about the people around us. Once you have individuals riding your energy bus, you must provide them appreciation and acknowledgment. Because it is in our nature to seek acknowledgment, you should make it a point to compliment outstanding work and positive energy.

We also need to have the awareness that our ultimate mission is frequently going to be much bigger than what it was that we initially set out to do. Therefore, it is important to maintain pliability and be open to new experiences and chances, as the environment around you is always shifting and developing. Because of our adaptability and resilience, we can take advantage of chances and make the most out of every circumstance.

The transformation that takes place in George by the end of the book is so profound that he has a 180-degree shift in both his vision and his worldview. His wife and family bathe in his sunny disposition, which contributes to the success of his marriage and home life.

In addition to this, following the success of George's work presentation, he informs his staff that they are free to go earlier than usual. But here's the thing: not a single one of them wants to go; rather, every one of them wants to stay and enjoy the celebration.

Because joy is an energy that can be shared and can present itself in the most profound ways, living a joyful life is not simply one person's tale; rather, it is a story that can become a collective one.

Made in the USA
Las Vegas, NV
27 September 2022